Salk Institute

Phaidon Press Limited
Regent's Wharf
All Saints Street
London N1 9PA

Phaidon Press, Inc
180 Varick Street
New York, NY 10014

www.phaidon.com

First published 1993
Reprinted 1996
This edition first published 2002
© 1993, 2002 Phaidon Press Limited
Photographs © 1993 Peter
Aprahamian except where stated
to the contrary

ISBN 0 7148 4214 1

A CIP catalogue record for this book
is available from the British Library

Printed in Hong Kong

The author acknowledges the role
of Dr Jonas Salk who provided
important information which was
necessary in the preparation of this
monograph, as well as that of Dianne
D. Carter of the public
relations department, and James Cox
of the photography department of the
Salk Institute. Dr Julia Moore
Converse at the Louis I Kahn
Collection, The Architectural
Archives, at the University of
Pennsylvania also provided kind
assistance in making drawings
available, to be included here with
redrawing carried out by Ann
Knudsen. He also expresses
gratitude to Victoria Turkel, at the
University of Southern California, who
researched various aspects of the
project.

     Text illustrations were kindly
provided by Grant Mudford (1); Louis
I. Kahn Collection, University of
Pennsylvania and Pennsylvania
Historical and Museum Commission,
copyright 1977 (6, 7, 14, 16, 17, 18,
19, 24 and 28); Ann Knudsen (8, 15)
and Kazi Khaleed Ashraf (49).

# Salk Institute
## Louis I Kahn

## James Steele
**ARCHITECTURE IN DETAIL**

When discussing how he received the commission for the Salk Institute for Biological Research near La Jolla, California, Louis Kahn was fond of telling the story of Dr Jonas Salk's visit to his office in Philadelphia in 1959. After a preliminary discussion, Kahn took Salk on a tour of the Richards Medical Research Building at the University of Pennsylvania, **1**, and was asked how many square feet the building provided. The fact that it was comparable in size to the project that Salk envisioned seemed to impress his potential client, and was to be the most specific initial piece of programmatic information he was to receive. Kahn had actually come to Salk's attention through a friend who had heard the architect deliver a speech entitled 'Order for Science and Art', related to the Richards towers, and the noted scientist had only intended to contact him for suggestions of names of other architects he might interview. The two got on so well that Salk felt he need look no further, **2, 3**.[1]

During their initial discussion, Kahn was also impressed by the fact that Salk wanted his laboratories to be the kind of place where 'Picasso could come to visit', and that medical research should not be confined to science alone. This image, of the humanization of science, and the possible unity of art and architecture struck a responsive chord in Kahn, for whom making the 'immeasurable measurable' continued to be a personal quest. As Kahn himself said, 'there was something else that he said which became the key to the entire space environment. Namely that medical research does not belong entirely to medicine or the physical sciences. It belongs to population. He meant that anyone with a mind in the humanities, in science, or in art could contribute to the mental environment of research, leading to discoveries in science. Without the restrictions of a dictatorial programme it became a rewarding experience to participate in the projection of an evolving programme of spaces without precedence'.[2]

In the first prospectus, produced by the Institute to generate capital for the new project, the far-sighted theme of health as a unitary, or holistic process is consistently stressed, as is the study of both the body and mind of the 'total person', **4**. To that end, it promotes a centre devoted to humane studies, and the inclusion of scholars in the belief that a study of 'a totality of values is integral to a vision of total health'.[3] The choice of the initial faculty of the Institute, which consisted of a distinguished group of resident and non-resident fellows working under Jonas Salk as President and Director, reflect this belief, **5**. In alphabetical order, these were Jacob Bronowski, Melvin Cohn, Francis Crick, Renato Dulbecco, Edwin Lennox, Jacques Monod, Leslie Orgel, Les Szilard and Warren Weaver. Implicit in this selection, particularly of the mathematician and humanist Bronowski, who contributed so much to the understanding of the place that science should occupy in modern culture, was a new attitude towards biological research, in which the humanities were not only seen to have a part, but in which physics and chemistry, traditionally seen as distinctly different studies, were now considered to be merged.[4]

### Three distinct phases

Early in 1960 Kahn visited La Jolla to help Salk determine how much land would be required for the project, and the City Council voted to contribute the site to the Institute in the spring of that year.[5] The first scheme was presented by Kahn in conjunction with the formal

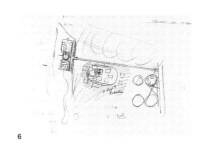

announcement of the project by Salk on March 15, 1960.[6] The residual influence of the Richards Medical Building is still evident, with the laboratories shown as clusters of towers near Torrey Pines Road. An intermediate zone, flanking the deep ravine that bisects the site is set aside for houses, designated as 'the Living Place', for the fellows on the south, and a recreation centre on the north. The 'Meeting Place', far out on the bluff overlooking the Pacific, is shown as having a narrow straight access road and a bridge of its own, and is rendered as a linear grouping positioned parallel to the face of the cliff. In it, lecture halls and an auditorium are organized around enclosed courts, all sharing an elongated ambulatory, intended to bring the scientists together, **6**, **7**. In a second version, which appeared nearly a year later, the vertical laboratory towers were replaced by four rectilinear, two-storey blocks set perpendicular to the sea. These are joined by a service area which completely separates them from the parking area and Torrey Pines Road, to the west. The central courts, around which each pair of laboratories are organized, were the result of Dr Salk's having mentioned his love of the monastery of St Francis of Assisi to Kahn, and a letter from the architect to Professor W.H. Jordy in August 1960, in which he mentions his intention to revisit the monastery himself, lends credence to its importance as the source of this idea, **8**.[7]

In their second configuration of 1961–62 the laboratories are made up of four clear span spaces, made possible by five box girders running across each rectangle, with a 'V'-shaped folded plate system perpendicular to the girders, spanning between them, **10–13**. Piping, threaded through the folded plates, is channelled into the box girders, to towers on the outside edge of each set of

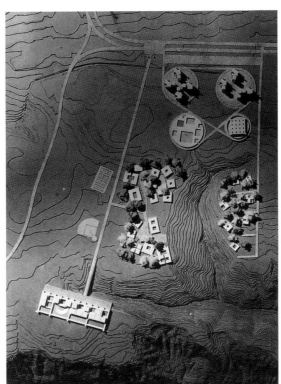
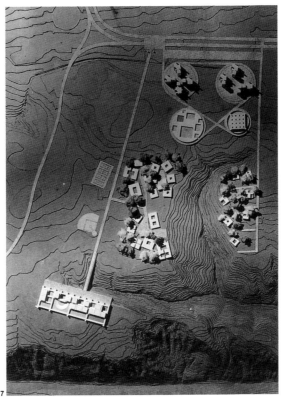

7

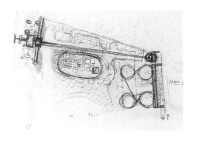

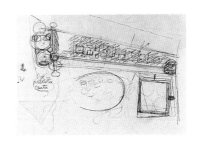

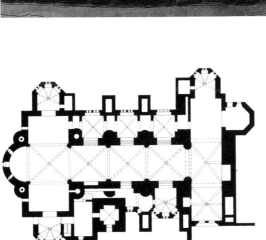

8

**9** The cliff-side site chosen by Salk and Kahn has spectacular views of the Pacific.
**10–12** Kahn's second scheme was based on two sets of laboratory blocks, each enclosing a planted, rectilinear central court, with both the Meeting Place and residences for the fellows adapted more closely to the contours of the cliff.
**13** Salk and Kahn discussing the second scheme.
**14** The American Consulate in Luanda was also an influential, environmental model for the Institute design.
**15** Hadrian's Villa, in Tivoli, inspired Kahn to 'wrap ruins' around the Meeting Place.
**16, 17** The Meeting Place, in its final configuration, was organized around a square, central hall.
**18** A central, pedestrian street, broken into small-scale segments by stairs between levels, was intended to serve as a spine for the residential group.

9

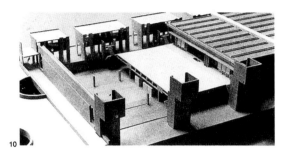

10

12

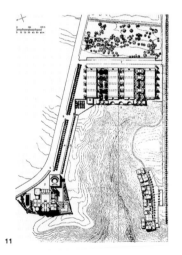

11

13

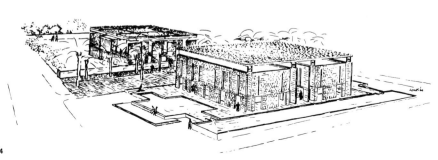

14

16

laboratories, used for exhaust. By turning the vertical duct shafts of the Richards Medical Building on their side, Kahn, the city architect not accustomed to such a large site, was beginning to respond to the expansiveness of the area available to him, as well as to pragmatic problems of dust on pipes which he had faced in the Research facility in Philadelphia. In addition to providing a relatively dust-free pipe chase, the folded plate system also allowed light to enter through the roof, as indicated in study models which show monitors punctured through the upper most set of Vs. The inequity, of allowing light into the top floor and not the bottom level of each two-storey laboratory block, because the second interior system could not be penetrated as well, may have been a factor in Kahn's agreeing to scrap the box girder and folded plate combination later on. The virtual inaccessibility of the pipes, and the need to have them make a 45 degree turn to run through the box girders to reach the exhaust towers, was the main reason given for the change.

In addition to the revision of the laboratories, the design of the Meeting Place in this scheme represents a significant departure for Kahn, as an extension of his 'theory of walls', first attempted in the American Consulate in Luanda, Angola, **14**, to counteract heat and glare. At a time when the main technological problem being addressed by modernism was how to make a glass curtain wall section thinner, Kahn was thinking about the space between the inner and outer surface and the possibility of separating the two. As he said: 'In the Salk project ... I am developing walls around buildings to take care of the glare. I do not think that venetian blinds and other kinds of window devices are architectural. They are department-store stuff and don't belong to architecture. The

architect must find an architecture out of glare, out of the wind, from which these shapes and dimensions are derived. And these glare walls are based on a very simple principle which I got… when I was in Africa. These walls I'm developing for the Salk Center in San Diego are in recognition of this discovery of the law of light'.[8]

Derived from Hadrian's Villa in Tivoli, **15**, the spaces in the second version of the Meeting Place, which include an auditorium, library, dining room and gymnasium, as well as guest quarters, are grouped around a covered hall, which is the ambulatory of the original scheme turned inward into a square, **16–18**.

**The final scheme**

After contracts were signed in the spring of 1962, Salk requested that Kahn simplify both the configuration of the laboratories, from four rectangular blocks to two, and the folded plate system which he felt was too inflexible.[9] Kahn concurred in the need for a reduction in the number of laboratories, but had hesitations about changing the structure writing that 'he felt the loss of the folded plate construction'.[10] The basic ideas of the 1961–62 scheme, of scientists' studies placed away from the laboratories in a central garden, and auxiliary spaces forming vertical towers on their external wall remained the same, but the architect increased the number of floors to three, with one of these below ground level. The five box girders spanning the width of the laboratories, and the 'V'-shaped folded plates running perpendicular to them, were replaced with thirteen Vierendeel beams, which create a 9 ft high service space above each of the three floors, allowing pipe chases to be dropped to the 65 x 245 ft floor below with more latitude than

17

18

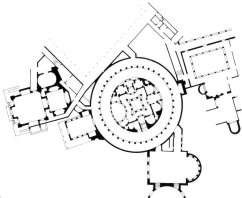

15

19

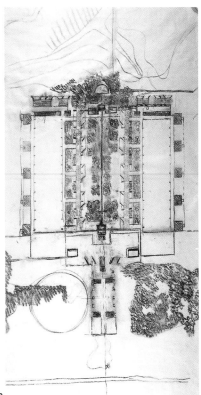

20

before. Mechanical rooms at the northern end of each rectangular block, and an extension for offices, overlooking the Pacific were also refined, but remain essentially the same as in the earlier plan, **19, 20**. The study towers, which now give the courtyard its distinctive, serrated edges, are called 'porticos of studies' in the final working drawings, indicating the architect's and client's intention that they serve as the arcade of the 'cloister' they both envisioned. These studies, which are grouped into pairs, align with the mechanical rather than laboratory floor levels, and are separated from them by bridges, in order to maintain a sufficient physical and psychological distance between the two. Each laboratory block has five study towers, with each tower containing four offices, except for those near the entrance to the court, which only contain two. A diagonal wall allows each of the thirty-six scientists using the studies to have a view of the Pacific, and every study is fitted with a combination of operable sliding and fixed glass panels in teak wood frames. The differentiation used in these windows, which is similar to that in the Esherick House in Chestnut Hill, is typical of Kahn, who believed that the purpose of fenestration should be clarified with the part used for natural light separated from grills for ventilation, **21–23**.

Another important change that took place in the design involved the central court, which Kahn had always visualized as a lush garden. By the time of substantial completion of the laboratories and studies in 1965, the architect had still not determined what form it should take, and after seeing an exhibit of Luis Barragán's work at the Museum of Modern Art in New York in that same year, Kahn wrote to him, with an offer to collaborate on the court. Barragán came to the Institute early in 1966, and as he later recalled, told Kahn

at first sight of the muddy field between the laboratories, 'Don't put one leaf nor plant, not one flower, nor dirt. Absolutely nothing – and I told him, a plaza… will unite the two buildings, and at the end, you will see the line of the sea. Lou was thinking, and stated a very important thing – that the surface is a facade that rises to the sky and unites the two as if everything had been hollowed out', **24, 25**.[11]

Dr Salk was not with the two when Barragán first shared this realization with Kahn, joining them a bit later in the court. He recalls that this idea was enthusiastically presented to him by both men, but that he felt some misgivings when Barragán described his cloister as a 'plaza for all nations', since he wanted it to be private.[12] The commissioning of landscape architect Lawrence Halprin, from San Francisco, in the late summer of 1966 indicates that these misgivings extended beyond metaphor, but Kahn eventually rejected additional embellishment, implementing Barragán's idea in the middle of 1967.[13]

In its final configuration, the Meeting Place seems to be the reciprocal of the laboratories, gaining in spontaneity what they have lost. In contrast to the second phase scheme, which is mostly rectilinear, with the exception of several semi-circular apses and redoubts, the third is a careful balance between the rational and the organic in which each element occupies its appropriate place in a thoughtful composition. The square theatre of the earlier plan has been replaced by a classical, fan-shaped proscenium, cut into the cliff, which introduces visitors to the complex. The square central hall, however, which diagrams the form necessary for meeting, remains, as does its open external equivalent overlooking the Pacific. The series of spaces surrounding the inner hall transform from cubes and towers on its northern and eastern edge, to circles in

21

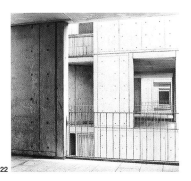

22

23

**19, 20** Following a
directive from Salk to
simplify the second
scheme, Kahn reduced
the four laboratory
blocks to two, flanking
a single, central court.
**21–23** Studies for the
scientists provide places
to escape from the
concentrated routine
of laboratory work; each
has shuttered windows
giving direct views to
the Pacific.
**24, 25** Kahn's continual
struggle to determine the
correct character of the
central court was finally
resolved by Barragan,
who advised that it be
free of landscaping.

24

25

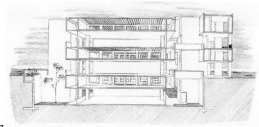

squares and squares in circles on the west and south, in a delightful volumetric translation of leeward and windward, sun and shadow, land and sea, with the plan resembling a diurnal freeze-frame diagram of a tree reacting to the light.

Little attention has thus far been given to the Living Place in the final scheme for the Institute, located directly across the ravine from the Meeting Place, to the north. In it, residences of various sizes were designed for research staff, scholarship holders and visitors in units that range from houses to apartments, as well as overnight accommodation and common areas. These are all placed on both sides of a central walkway, with parking provided on the exterior, southern edge. The residences step down on four levels of equal length as the internal street approaches the Pacific, breaking down the impression of distance, and giving the entire complex the intimate scale of a small village, **26–28**. A loop in the contours of the ravine closer to the laboratories would seem to have been a more desirable location for direct access and a more compact massing of residences, and when asked about this Kahn once again raised the important issue of distance, which had already proven to be so vexing in establishing the location of the studies. Answering a question with a question he responded by asking: 'How far is too far, how near is too near?' in typical Socratic fashion.[14] This sense of a retreat far enough away from the main place of work, which had also governed the choice of the position of the Meeting Place, was the main factor in the choice of the location of the residences, and views up and down the coast was another. As described by Brownlee and DeLong: 'In the third version of the houses for fellows, revised for the last time during the early months of 1962,

seven different types of two-storey buildings equipped with ample porches and balconies lined both sides of a narrow pedestrian street. Together they could accommodate more than fifty residents and guests. At either end, two-bedroom houses shared small plazas with adjacent guest quarters – the larger and more spacious of these was located at the western edge overlooking the ocean'.[15]

The possible realization of the Living Place at this point is even more problematic and unlikely than that of its meeting component, opposite. Speculative housing at this edge of the property has now completely changed the character of this part of the site, so that the ocean views of the southern half of the complex are now blocked, and the spirit of the concept has been compromised.

In their final detailing and materials, the laboratories, as built, reflect the architect's careful concern, evident in the design of all parts of the Institute.

### Concrete

In determining the mix to be used in the concrete, which is the major material of the laboratory complex, and also intended to be used in the Living and Meeting Places, Kahn researched the components used in Roman pozzolana, in order to achieve a similar, reddish hue. He paid close attention to the forms, which were made of ¾ in exterior plywood, filled and sanded, and finished with coats of catalysed polyurethane resin. These were able to be used as many as eight times before being repaired and refinished.[16]

Rather than try to hide the joints between the panels, which would have resulted in some spalling, Kahn decided to accentuate them, chamfering the edges to produce a V-shaped groove at these

**26–28** The studies, on which Kahn lavished much care, are located directly across from the interstitial mechanical space, rather than the laboratories, in order to provide more privacy. **29** Dr Salk readily attributes the choice of site, with its dramatic juxtaposition of sea and sky, to Kahn. **30–33** Due to the close interrelationship between building and ground, a great deal of excavation was required during construction.

31

30

32

33

34–36 Salk shared Kahn's enthusiasm for exposed concrete and became involved in the final approval process, checking colour and detailing of subterranean walls prior to the placement of those above them.

37 Structural diagram illustrating the principle of post-tensioning the columns; tension bars similar to those in the columns are also threaded through the bottom chord of each of the trusses to provide earthquake resistance.

34

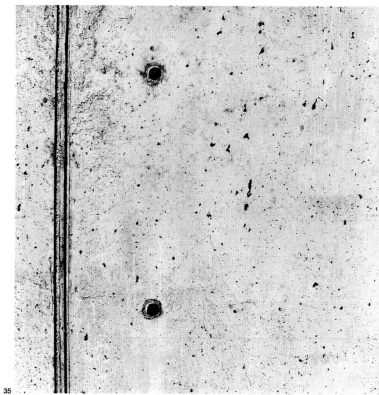

35

points along the wall surface, **34**. To avoid leakage and bleeding, the contractor used solid corners and gasketed joints between sets of gauged forms.[17] The conical holes left by the form ties were also not patched, so their spacing was carefully considered, and they were filled by a lead plug, hammered tightly into each to prevent corrosion of the steel ties, **35**.

Dr Salk was particularly interested in the colour and quality of the concrete and became involved in the approval of test walls, which would eventually form retaining walls, which would be covered with fill and not be visible. He, along with Kahn, rejected several batches before the final mix was accepted, **36**.

### Structure

Stringent seismic criteria related to construction in the San Diego area made it difficult for Kahn's structural engineer, August E Komendant, to convince local building officials, who wanted him to use a steel frame, that a concrete, Vierendeel truss system would have the required flexibility. They agreed only after Komendant had submitted a report containing over 400 pages of doubly integrated deflection computations that demonstrated that post-tensioned columns would provide the main resistance to lateral seismic forces. These columns, which absorb both dead and live load compression plus vertical post-tensioning forces, have been designed to maintain zero tension if subjected to lateral movements of the kind delivered by earthquakes. The vertical ends of the 9 foot deep trusses, which are spaced 20 feet on centre and have a clear span of 65 feet, alternate with the columns to form the integral, vertical support of the building. The stress steel bars, which were

progressively post-tensioned against wedge anchor plates at the top of each truss as construction proceeded, were coated with asphalt paint and inserted in metal conduit to prevent bonding with the concrete. Three of these bars, similarly painted and encased, are draped through the bottom chord of each of the 18 foot wide trusses, acting like elastic 'tendons' that will elongate if an earthquake should occur, **37**. In this way, Komendant was able to provide a building which has twice the amount of controlled ductility of a steel structure of comparable size.[18]

As described in issues of *Engineering News-Record* released while construction was still under way: 'The trusses' bottom chords are post-tensioned, with the tendons slightly draped through the end panels to help resist the reaction shear. Unlike the column tendons, the truss tendons are grouted in their flexible steel conduits. The top chord of the vertical web members are reinforced. Each truss was cast in two sections, with a construction joint at the top plane of the bottom chords. Since the bottom-chord concrete merely serves as a protective cover for the post-tensioning cables, the cross section of the bottom chord is much shallower, and thus more flexible than the top chord, which must resist compressive forces with a combination of concrete and reinforcing steel … thus resulted the requirement for a monolithic casting of the web members of the top chord'.[19]

### Building services

The sophistication of the mechanical systems is in keeping with the general philosophy of flexibility and reliability applied by Kahn in the design of the building itself. A high-temperature water system was

**36**

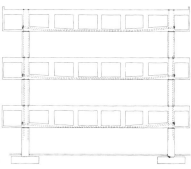

**37**

**38** As might be
expected in a building
requiring such careful
environmental control,
the HVAC systems
are very complex.
**39** Final installation
of the shutters for
the studies.

**40, 41** Kahn freely
admitted his dislike
of exposed pipes; his
provision of large
mechanical spaces
between the laboratory
floors allows them
to be hidden.

39

chosen instead of steam as the main energy source for the central plant of the Institute. By submitting hot water to a pressure of 200psi, it *can* be heated to 350°F without flashing to vapour, allowing for high levels of energy without the maintenance problems that usually accompany steam systems. High-temperature water is produced in the plant by a combination of natural gas-fired boilers, plus jacket water heat and exhaust gas heat from cogeneration engines. The heated water is then distributed to various building systems where it discharges its energy to produce space heating, space cooling, domestic hot water and steam for laboratory sterilizers, in a simple, low-maintenance energy system derived from a central source. Redundancy, which gives every mechanical system enough capacity for one on-line unit, with one on stand-by, gives service staff the ability to perform routine maintenance on almost all plant equipment without interrupting service.

Because research activity goes on all day, the heating, ventilating and air-conditioning systems must also remain in operation constantly. Ventilation is required to be 100% fresh air since the potential hazards of the laboratory environment prohibit re-circulation. The minimum number of air changes per hour is twelve. The North Building utilizes a 'dual duct system' for its heating and cooling. Two separate supply air ducts have been installed. One is heated with a central re-heat coil, while the other is cooled with a central chilled water coil to between 55 and 60°F. Local zoned thermostats then regulate mechanical dampers which mix the hot and cold air supplied to each zone to maintain required room temperatures. The South Building uses a different heating and cooling design, called a 're-heat system', in which only a cold air

duct, cooled by a central chilled water coil, is necessary. The chilled water used to cool both the north and south cold air ducts is generated in absorption-type chilling units which operate on a chemical cycle, as opposed to a mechanical or Freon-type cycle. A 233 ton absorber is sufficient most of the year, but during the hot summer months, one or both 750 ton absorbers are used.

The electrical service, provided by three separate power sources, guarantees a reliable supply to the Institute. The normal source is the local utility company circuit 245 which enters the Institute from the north. An alternative is circuit 65, entering from the south. A third power service, which is synchronized with these two utility circuits, is an in-house co-generation plant, which has two 650KW units driven by 940 HP reciprocating engines. These are capable of meeting base requirements but utility power must be used to supplement their output at periods of peak demand during the working-day. By generating most of its own electrical power, the Institute has not only greatly reduced its utility bills, but has also reduced the possibility of a sustained power outage, which would threaten vital work in progress. As added insurance against this, there are two small emergency generators which are set to start up automatically if there is a power shortage. There are additional systems, necessary to a research laboratory, which have been provided, such as a 2,000 gallon-per-day reverse osmosis system that provides high-quality distilled water to each laboratory sink. After reverse osmosis, the water is sent through charcoal filters and resin polishing bottles to purify it further, before it is held in stainless steel storage tanks. It is then pumped through a closed-loop circulating system, to prevent it from stagnation before being tapped at

laboratory outlets. Compressed air, used in laboratory incubators, is provided by two reciprocating compressors that send it through an after-cooler to remove condensed moisture before it passes through a second stage of air-drying in a refrigeration-type dryer. This dried, compressed air is then delivered at 40psi through the interstitial space piping to its point of use in the laboratories. Steam is also needed for sterilization purposes. It is produced via two steam generators from energy available in the high temperature hot water loop. After it is used for sterilization, the steam condenses, and the condensate is pumped back to the central plant, where it is either recycled into the steam generators once again, or dumped into drains, depending on its water quality. Natural gas, diesel fuel, liquefied carbon dioxide and special gases are also available for use by researchers, completing the list of services to the laboratories, **38**.[20]

It is useful to describe these systems in detail not just because the complex function of the project suggests it, but also because the thoughtful provisions made for them belie Kahn's general reputation, in some quarters, as an impractical dreamer, who frequently overlooked such details. While he was undoubtedly assisted by a very talented team of consultants, the decision to shift from a folded plate to Vierendeel structure was ultimately his alone. As he said, in connection with the University of Pennsylvania Medical Laboratories: 'I do not like ducts; I do not like pipes. I hate them really thoroughly, but because I hate them so thoroughly, I feel they have to be given their place. If I just hated them and took no care, I think they would invade the building and completely destroy it. I want to correct any notion you may have that I am in love with that kind of thing', **40, 41**.[21]

38

40

41

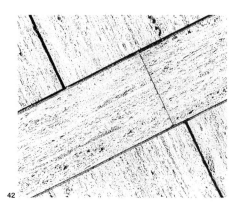

42

## Critical evaluation

Louis Kahn embodied the critical method in both practice and teaching, to the extent that he had one full-time member of staff available for discussions on the progress of each of his projects at all times. He encouraged objective analysis and would welcome, rather than be offended by, relevant evaluations that have been made in the three decades since the completion of an institute generally regarded as his masterpiece. The most consistent, and positive part of that commentary has been the value of the foresight shown in making allowances for flexibility and change in the laboratories in an integral, rather than superficial way, through the provision of 'interstitial' spaces for mechanical services, **44**. While considered by some to be financially and spatially excessive when built, these have proven to be viable, repaying their original cost many times over.

Equivalent to this in a more general sense was Kahn's distinction between 'form' and 'design', which differed from the general understanding of these terms. As Marshall Meyers, who worked with him has explained: 'He talked about "design" and "form" often. To him design was the "how" and form was the "what". Design was those things which were personal, which were his: the colours he liked, his love of natural materials, his preference for certain proportions and shapes. Form was what to do. He searched for realizations which, if found, would belong to everyone'.[22]

Form, for Kahn, also had an 'existence will', and the architect's role was to allow it to manifest itself with as little hindrance as possible, so that personality, technique and trend would not dominate. The 'realizations' that Marshall Meyers speaks of were those that were fundamental to human nature, to the extent of even being above the cultural differences which design should answer to. The materials used in the Salk project, then, while expressive of such a search, are a function of choice, and have proven to be especially prescient, setting this project outside the usual considerations of style and fashion to which others are constantly exposed.

Kahn frequently spoke of a 'timeless' architecture, and of discovering 'what has always been, and what will always be'. His diverse historical interests, from Roman engineering techniques to Scottish castles, were all related to this idea of enduring institutions and durable transcendent forms that were above whim and fancy. His concrete here has a pozzolana additive not only intended to soften its appearance, but to make a symbolic connection through time to the origins of this composite material. Slate, which was the first choice for the central courtyard because of its striking contrast with the concrete, and its ability to convey the sombre dimension of an institution engaged in a constant struggle against life-threatening diseases, was eliminated because of cost, and replaced with travertine, which has similar symbolic connections. Because of its relative softness, the travertine has not lasted as well as the slate may have over time, but has proven to be a perfect visual and tactile foil to the concrete walls. Teak, used as latticework screening in the scientists' studies facing into the court, was similarly believed to be financially excessive by many at first, but in a subtle detail characteristic of this architect, was left unvarnished, to weather naturally, further reducing maintenance. Each decision

in the design, made in this way, has ensured longevity in an endeavour increasingly fraught with the risk of renovation or demolition, **42, 43**.

The Institute has fared equally well in broad considerations of function, with the exception of its main entrance and the clarity of circulation throughout. In a critique written shortly after the completion of the complex, Stanford Anderson was one of the first to note that, in the radical change that occurred between the first and last schemes, Kahn's original intention of having a 'non-hierarchical, semi-continuous series of units stretched across the site, translating between the private domain of the dwellings and the public and ideologically central meeting house' was lost.[23] Implied in that loss was the impossibility of any scientist now simply being more than 'the first among equals' in a community of scholars engaged in a common pursuit. The symmetry of the final design, which has resulted from several very plausible concerns expressed by Dr Salk, about the inherent possibility of competition between people working in different sets of buildings each centred around their own courtyard, as well as undue cost, which was accepted by Kahn as having greater clarity, was nonetheless imposed upon his original form realization and has changed it.

As Anderson has said: 'The approach from the east presents the visitor with the hard and bleak symmetry of the monumental stairs and the (from this view) windowless concrete buildings. Since the central feature of this symmetry is a void, the visitor is neither positively received nor is it possible … to know which way to turn. The sense of an impending wrong decision is intensified by the over split in the site which becomes more emphatic as one

43

**42, 43** Careful detailing
of a limited palette
of basic materials
projects a final, overall
impression of strength
and durability.
**44** The interstitial
mechanical spaces
that Kahn provided

allow for flexible
and uncluttered
laboratory floors.
**45** A televised
discussion between
Jonas Salk and several
of the original resident
fellows, in a mock-up
of one of the studies.

44

45

looks west…'.[24] In Anderson's view, the obvious expedient of a closure across the eastern end of the laboratories would be equally unsatisfactory because it defeats the sense of continuity along the north–south axis that was always Kahn's intention, and irrevocably establishes this hierarchical, bilateral condition as a constant.[25]

The preparation, over a seven-year period, of such a scheme by a California office, and its imminent construction have made this a particularly sensitive and controversial question, confirming its importance as an unresolved issue. On the other hand, there is a powerful impression conveyed by the open front door of the Institute, as finally realized, that can only be compared to the discovery of a hidden ruin, where the line of demarcation between building and nature is clearly drawn. As in Ostia or Phaesilis, where a single extended footstep is the only measure between a forest floor cushioned with pine needles and a paved Decumanus lined with partially recognizable structures on either side, the move upward through a small wood onto the central court of the Institute is as deliberately elemental as the architecture itself, the certitude of a conventional 'reception hall' replaced with a sense of anticipation and discovery now rare in an increasingly sterilized and predictable world, **46**.

There is, finally, the constant awareness that this is an incomplete dream, missing its most vital component. The Meeting Place, on which Kahn lavished so much love, and which he saw as the antithesis of the laboratories, and an irreplaceable component of the entire project, has never been realized, halted by Dr Salk on the pretext of design 'premise', rather than lack of funds, which was the real reason. It was to be the embodiment of the ideal of unity expressed in the original mission statement of the Institute. While the residential portion of the complex may arguably have been omitted without serious damage to the form idea, the loss of the Meeting Place has seriously compromised it, to the great detriment of the institution. This loss is felt at several levels, most poignantly in the lack of any communal space except for a reception area, **47**, and auditorium, **48**, in the South Building which might begin to approximate to such a function in the laboratories. The expansive talent of Jacob Bronowski, for whom the Meeting Place would have been the perfect mileau in which to discuss the cultural implications of science, was wasted within the one-dimensional restrictions of the laboratory, where research, not philosophy, is the main priority, and others, with his broad perspective, have not followed him. Another level of the realization of loss is historical, in that an important stage in Kahn's intellectual evolution, regarding the space existing inside structure, bracketed as it has been by the Embassy in Luanda and the Assembly Building in Bangladesh, **49**, has not been physically transcribed. Dr Salk still maintains that the Meeting Place may yet be built, but since attention and financial resources have now been focused on the construction of a reception hall at the opposite end of the site, the probability of this happening seems increasingly remote.

## Kahn's legacy

If the laboratories may be referred to as the lungs of the Salk Institute, the Meeting Place was to be its brain, and the body is incomplete. It was not a direct request of the client, but a desire inferred by a

47

48

49

**50, 51** The power of the
final design is directly
attributable to the close
collaboration that took
place between client
and architect, and the
respect that each had
for the other.

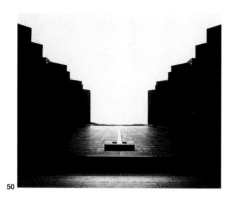

50

particularly intuitive architect from every word and gesture he was able to respond to, including the final configuration of the site itself. As Kahn once said: 'Need stands for what is already present, and it becomes a kind of measurement of the already present. Desire becomes a sense of the not yet made. That is the main difference between need and desire … the architectural programme that comes to you then, becomes transformed, because you see the needs in it, and you see that which has not been expressed in the inspirations you feel. The society of spaces talking to each other in a plan is what reveals itself as an architectural validity, a harmony discovered out of the mere areas in a programme'.[26] Without the Meeting Place, the harmony evident in Kahn's final plan regrettably remains unfulfilled.

After Kahn's death in 1975, there was a great deal of speculation about his place in history, which, at this remove, now seems secure. The part played by the Salk Institute in establishing that place, in both concept and realization is substantial, because it marks a point of integration irrespective of questions related to translation of form. Ironically the exploration of internal, structural space, which is indicated so clearly in the layering between the inside and outside walls of the Meeting Place was soon to be redirected into an identifiable style which, at its best, retained something of the joyfulness contained in Kahn's contemporary translation of the Maritime Theatre, but at its worst was a vehicle for impermanent facadisim, at the opposite extreme to his eternal architecture. At the height of its popularity, Michael Graves, who did as much as Robert

Venturi and Charles Moore in promoting it, said that: 'If we should regard one figure as responsible for the turn of events that we are now experiencing in architecture as a move away from the modern movement, it would have to be Louis Kahn. Certainly there were and are documents such as "Complexity and Contradiction" that bring us to a conscious level of understanding of the breadth of things that were being missed by modern architecture in the academic sense, but in terms of the work alone, Lou was the first to say, wait a minute, that isn't the only answer … we've been struggling with this idea of technology for so long now of making the walls thinner and thinner, lets look at it a different way. In a way what many people are doing now – whatever we call it – would not have taken the same route if it hadn't been for Lou's work … In the stylistic sense I don't think that's true. I don't think that he is very influential today'.[27]

The subsequent failure of post-modernism to establish a durable, perpetuating language, is precisely *why* Kahn's influence was not discernible in the style, and the recent renewal of interest in his work, particularly among students who have grown weary of trying to decipher charts that purport to trace all of the variants that have followed since, is indicative of his ability to rise above style. Students crowded into lecture halls to listen to this diminutive, charismatic man, who spoke in a poetry they could only partially understand, because they had finally discovered someone who spoke about order, permanence and timelessness. Such things are rarely discussed in schools today, but the students' desire to talk about them remains strong, especially at a time when the belief in institutions is fading.

The international mixture of students in Kahn's Masters class at the University of Pennsylvania, under the leadership of Dean G Holmes Perkins, who had been given a mandate in 1951 to expand the curriculum of the School to include the totality of the man-made and natural environment, ensured the dissemination of graduates with a more contextual view toward architecture, who took these ideas back to their respective countries. While widely touted as a principle of post-modernism, the perfect fit between building and place, seen in such examples as Stirling's Staatsgalerie in Stuttgart, is very rare, and yet contextualism, or 'Critical Regionalism' as Kenneth Frampton calls it, has survived the death of the style, emerging now with localized agendas of its own.

Kahn discussed his work at length in his design studio, and since the Salk Institute occupied him for six years, from 1959 to 1965, it, along with the Assembly Hall in Bangladesh, and the Indian Institute of Management in Ahmedabad, had an enormous influence on a large number of students. They absorbed the lessons that each had to offer, especially about adaptation to site, climate and culture. Poised as it is at the juncture of land, sea and sky, the La Jolla project strikes a responsive chord in the American psyche as a calliper of the furthest extent of western expansion, on its precipice above the Pacific. Like the early Missions in this region, it acknowledges the need for closure in a windswept landscape, compromised by the open axis from east to west. The cloisters of those Missions, as well as their massive walls and deep-set, shuttered windows, were a response to nearly continuous sunshine which, while mostly benign, in combination with ocean breezes, is deceptively strong, with a high degree of glare. Kahn was absorbed with the question of the meaning of light, which here is ambivalently presented as both the source of life and the means of its destruction. The story of the evolution of the laboratories is one of both simplification and reduction, with the central courtyard transformed from a microcosmic paradisaical garden, as it is in the Alhambra, into a horizontal, reflective façade, open to the sky. His choice of materials, on the other hand, takes the harmful effects of light, as well as the corrosive action of salt air into consideration, since each is the most durable and yet vital option possible for its expressed purpose.

Kahn often attempted to describe the creative instinct through reference to its genetic source, frequently using a bilateral diagram, in which the words 'Silence and Light' were written on either side of a central, axial line. The primal necessity of light is implicit in this reduction, and he insisted that it be considered a generating force in all of his architecture. The Salk Institute changes in aspect during each hour of the day, depending on solar angle and the shadows that are cast, but is most memorable at sunset, when the horizon becomes a fiery wall at the end of the court. For this last hour it is the physical embodiment of Kahn's diagram, the closest he has ever come to realizing 'chapter zero' in any of his work, fully allowing for all of the new discoveries that have followed.

51

## Notes

**1** David B. Brownlee and David G. DeLong, *Louis I. Kahn: In the Realm of Architecture*, New York, p.330.

**2** Louis Kahn, *Writings, Lectures, Interviews*, New York, 1991, p.118.

**3** Salk Institute Prospectus, 1959, p.8.

**4** Statement by Dr Warren Weaver delivered at the Biltmore Hotel, New York, May 6 1963.

**5** Brownlee and DeLong, op. cit., p.330.

**6** ibid. p.330.

**7** Heinz Ronner and Sharad Shaveir, *Louis I. Kahn: Complete Works 1935–1974*, Boston, 1967, p.133.

**8** Kahn, op. cit., p.150.

**9** Ronner and Shaveir, op. cit., p.141.

**10** Kahn, op. cit., p.207.

**11** Brownlee and DeLong, op. cit., p.441.

**12** Jonas Salk's address to the ACSA Technology Conference in San Diego, 1992.

**13** Brownlee and DeLong, op. cit., p.441.

**14** Louis Kahn's lecture to the Masters class, University of Pennsylvania, 1969.

**15** Brownlee and DeLong, op. cit., p.444.

**16** Salk Institute public relations brochure, p.3.

**17** ibid. p.4.

**18** Technical Bulletin Stress Steel Corporation, August 1966, Bulletin No. 21, p.1.

**19** *Engineering News-Record*, January 27 1966, p.6.

**20** Salk Institute public relations brochure, p.10.

**21** Richard Saul Wurman and Eugene Feldman (eds) *The Notebooks and Drawings of Louis I. Kahn*, Philadelphia, 1962.

**22** *Architecture and Urbanism: Louis I. Kahn: Conception and Meaning*, A+U Publishing, 1983, p.224.

**23** Stanford Anderson, 'Louis I. Kahn in the 1960's', *Boston Society of Architects Journal*, 1, 1967, p.27.

**24** ibid. p.28.

**25** ibid. p.29.

**26** John Cook and Heinrich Klotz, *Conversations with Architects*, New York, 1973, p.180.

**27** *A+U*, op. cit., p.220.

## Specifications

Date of completion: July 1965

Dimension of each laboratory: 245ft (length) x 65ft (width)

Laboratory ceiling height: 11ft

Height of interstitial space: 9ft

Number and spacing of Vierendeels: 13 per building at 20ft centres

Dimension of courtyard: 270ft x 90ft

Size of light wells: 40ft x 25ft

Aluminium service slots: 4ft 8in (length) x 10ft (width) @ 5ft O.C.

Total gross square footage including all auxiliary structures: 411,580 sq ft

Structural Engineer: August E. Komendant

Structural Consultant: Ferver Dorland and Associates, Associated Structural Engineers, San Diego, CA

Laboratory Design Consultants: Early L. Walls Associates, La Jolla, CA

Site Engineer: Rick Engineers Co., San Diego, CA

Landscaping: Roland S. Hoyt, San Diego, CA

Landscape Consultant: Luis Barragan, Mexico City, Mexico

General Contractor: George A. Fuller Co., New York City

Mechanical and Electrical: University Mechanical and Engineering Contractors Inc., San Diego, CA; Fred S. Dubin Associates, New York City; Capital Electric Co., San Diego, CA

Job Captain for Louis Kahn: Jack MacAllister

Courtyard paving: travertine marble

Metalwork: A242 steel

## Bibliography

'Academic ratrace', *Architectural Review*, 139, March 1966, pp.168–9.

'Address by Louis I. Kahn: April 5, 1966', *Boston Society of Architects Journal*, 1967, pp.7–20.

**Anderson, Stanford**, 'Louis I. Kahn in the 1960s', *Boston Society of Architects Journal*, 1, 1967, pp.21–30.

**Andrews, Wayne**, *Architecture in America*, New York, 1977, p.161.

**Borck, F.K.**, 'Planung mit Installationsgeschossen Dargestellt an Bauten des Cesundheitswesens in Usa and Kanada', *Bauwelt*, 64, June 18 1963, p.1033.

**Frampton, Kenneth**, *Modern Architecture: A Critical History*, Cambridge and New York, 1980, pp.244–6.

**Guirgola, Romaldo**, *Louis I. Kahn*, Boulder, Colorado, 1975, pp.60, 66–75.

**Hall, Mary Harrington**, 'Gifts from the sea and the high hopes of Jonas Salk', *San Diego Magazine*, 14 February 1962, pp.41–5, 105–6.

**Hammett, Ralph Warner**, *Architecture in the United States: A Survey of Architectural Styles Since 1776*, New York, p.306.

**Harms, Hans H.**, 'Trends in Architektur: USA-Louis I. Kahn', *Bauwelt*, 54, October 28 1963, pp.1252–61.

**Hughes, Robert**, 'Building with spent light', *Time*, January 15 1973, pp.60–65.

**Hughes, Robert**, 'Brick is stingy, concrete is generous: Salk Institute', *Horizon*, 16, Autumn 1974, pp.36–7.

**Jencks, Charles**, *Modern Movements in Architecture*, Garden City, New York, 1973, pp.213–33.

'Jonas Salk: der Sinn des Menschen fur Ordnung', *Werk*, July 1974.

**Jordy, William H.**, 'Symbolic essence of modern European architecture of the twenties and its continuing influence', *Society of Architectural Historians*, 22 October 1963, pp.186–7.

**Kahn, Louis, I.**, 'Form and Design', *Architectural Design*, April 1961, pp.152–4.

**Kahn, Louis, I.**, *The Notebooks and Drawings of Louis Kahn*, edited and designed by Richard Saul Wurman and Eugene Feldman, Philadelphia, 1962, pp.48–61.

**Kahn, Louis, I.**, 'Remarks', *Perspecta*, 9/10, 1965, pp.332–5.

**Kahn, Louis, I.**, *Drawings*, Los Angeles, 1981, pp.27–32.

'Kahn not for the faint-hearted', *AIA Journal*, 55, June 1971, pp.28–9.

**Komendant, August E.**, *18 Years with Architect Louis I. Kahn*, Englewood, New York, 1975, pp.41–73.

'Laboratory 1: precession of massive forms', *Architectural Forum*, 122, May 1965, pp.36–45.

'Labs Slab', *Architectural Review*, 143, March 1968, pp.173–4.

**Lobell, John**, *Between Silence and Light*, Boulder, Colorado, 1979, pp.7, 25, 34, 76–85.

'Louis I. Kahn exhibit', *Arts and Architecture*, 82, July 1965, pp.36–7.

'Louis I. Kahn; Oeuvres 1963–1969', *Architecture d'Aujourd'hui*, 142, February–March 1969, pp.80–87, 100.

'Louis Kahn', *Architecture d'Aujourd'hui*, 33, December 1962, pp.29–34.

'Louis Kahn: en Ameridansk Arkitekt', *Arkitekten*, 8, August 1966, pp.149–60.

'Louis Kahn: Institut Salk', *Architecture d'Aujourd'hui*, January 1967, pp.4–10.

**Maki, Fumihiko**, 'Kahn, Louis, I., Richards Medical Research Building, Pennsylvania 1961, Salk Institute for Biological Studies, California, 1965'. Edited and photographed by Yukio Futagawa. *Global Architecture*, 5, 1971, pp.9–25.

**McCoy, Esther**, 'Buildings in the United States: 1966–1967', *Lotus*, 4, 1967–8, pp.50–57.

**McCoy, Esther**, 'Dr. Salk talks about his Institute', *Architectural Forum*, 127, December 1967, pp.27–35.

**Magnago Lampugnani, Vittorio**, *Architecture of the 20th Century in Drawings*, New York, 1982, p.162.

**Mee, Charles L.**, 'Louis Kahn', *Three Centuries of Notable American Architects* (ed. Joseph J. Thorndike), New York, 1981, pp.288–9, 292, 294.

'The mind of Louis Kahn', *Architectural Forum*, 127, July–August 1972, pp.42, 45, 85–87.

**Nairn, Janet**, 'Conference dissects works of five very different architects', *Architecture*, 73, October 1984, pp.16, 18, 21.

'An old master's footnote preserves an early idea', *Fortune*, 74, July 1966, p.126.

**Pierson, William Harvey**, *American Buildings and Their Architects: The Impact of European Modernism in the Mid-Twentieth Century*, Vol 4, Garden City, New York, 1972, pp.383–7, 389–90, 411–12.

**Ragon, Michel**, 'Power of Doubt', *Connaissance des Arts*, December 1980, pp.84–91.

**Ronner, Heinz**, *Louis I. Kahn: Complete Works, 1935–74*, Boulder, Colorado, 1977, pp.143–67.

**Roth, Leland M.**, *A Concise History of American Architecture*, 1979, pp.301–3.

**Roth, Ueli**, 'Zwei Forschungslabratorian', *Werk*, 54, April 1967, pp.193–204.

**Rowan, Jan C.**, 'Wanting to be; the Philadelphia School', *Progressive Architecture*. April 1961, pp.142–9.

'Il Salk Institute di Louis Kahn', *Architettura*, 11, November 1965, pp.462–3.

'Salk Institute for Biological Studies', *Architecture + Urbanism*, January 1973, pp.28–9, 61, 79–88.

'Salk Institute for Biological Studies, La Jolla (San Diego)', *Werk*, July 1974, pp.804–5.

'Salk Institute, La Jolla', *World Architecture*, 4, 1967, pp.40–47.

**Scully, Vincent**, *Louis I. Kahn*, New York, 1962, p.36.

**Scully, Vincent**, 'Light, form and power, new work of Louis Kahn', *Architectural Forum*, 121, August–September 1964, p.166.

**Scully, Vincent**, 'Recent works by Louis Kahn', *Zodiac*, 17, 1967, pp.80–103.

**Scully, Vincent**, *American Architecture and Urbanism*, New York, 1969, pp.221–2.

**Smith, G.E. Kidder**, *A Pictorial History of Architecture in America*, New York, 1976, pp.818–19.

**Smith, G.E. Kidder**, *The Architecture of the United States*, Garden City, New York, 1981, pp.94–7.

**Stern, Robert A.M.**, *New Directions in American Architecture*, New York, 1969, pp.19–21. Revised 1977.

**Temko, Allan**, 'Evaluation: Louis Kahn's Salk Institute after a dozen years; what it is and what it might have been', *AIA Journal*, 66, March 1977, pp.42–9.

'Ten buildings that point to the future', *Fortune*, 72, December 1965, pp.174–5, 178.

**Tentori, Francesco**, 'Il passato come un amico', *Casabella*, 275, May 1963, pp.34–40.

**Tyng, Alexandra**, *Beginnings: Louis I. Kahn's Philosophy of Architecture*, New York, 1984, pp.40–43, 74–5, 140–42, 147–8, 165.

'Ulkomaat', *Arkkitehti*, February 1974, p.23.

**Weeks, John**, 'A design approach' in *Design for Research; Principles of Laboratory Architecture* (ed. Susan Braybooke), pp.4–8.

**West, Don**, 'Doctor Salk's bold new venture', *Pagent Magazine*, February 1962, pp.156–61.

**Whiffen, Marcus**, *American Architecture, 1606–1976*, Cambridge, Mass., 1981, pp.426–33.

**Wilson, Richard Guy**, 'Gold Medal for 1971; Louis Isadore Kahn', in *The AIA Gold Medal*, New York, 1984, pp.123, 212.

Photographs

Paving and joint lines
in the concrete have
considerable importance
in adding scale to what
might otherwise have
been severe surfaces.

A line of water beginning
at the entrance and
running the entire
length of the courtyard,
culminates in a fountain
at its western end,
symbolic of the
Pacific nearby.

The projecting studies,
like the cloister of a
monastery, cast deep
shadows into an arcade.
Following spread,
diagonal elements
projecting out from
the studies were a
specific request of
Dr Salk, who wanted
each scientist to have
a view of the ocean.

Employing very
straightforward means,
Kahn has provided
seemingly infinite
juxtapositions of forms
that are a constant
source of delight.

Durable materials have
ensured the longevity
of the complex in such
harsh climatic conditions.

The travertine paving in
the central court is also
used on stair treads.

Below left, exterior
view of the library.
Right, Kahn saw the
studies as 'the place
of the oak table and
the fireplace', where the
routine of the laboratory
could be momentarily
left behind.

The Salk Institute is the
embodiment of Kahn's
idea of silence and light.

**Site plan**

(prior to final revision)

**1** laboratory group 1
and central court

**2** laboratory group 2
and central court

**3** holding pen

**4** residences for
fellows and visitors

**5** residence parking

**6** meeting place

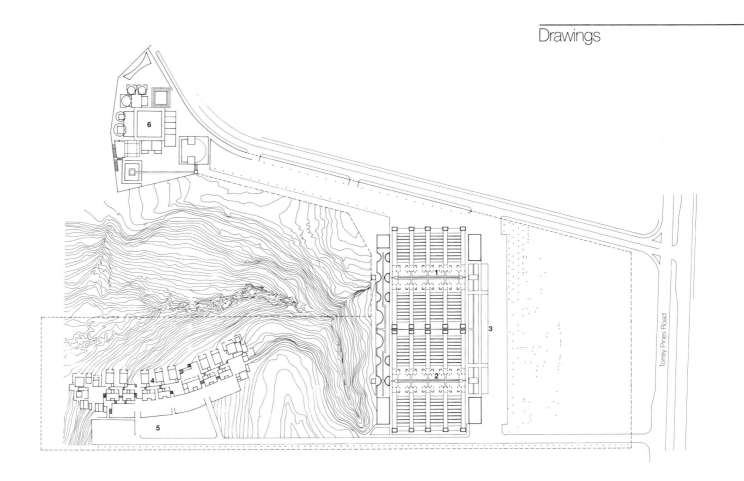

0          100 metres

0          100 yards

**Site plan**

(as built)

**1** north laboratory

**2** studies

**3** central court

**4** south laboratory

**5** visitor parking

**6** staff parking

**7** auxiliary services

**8** mechanical

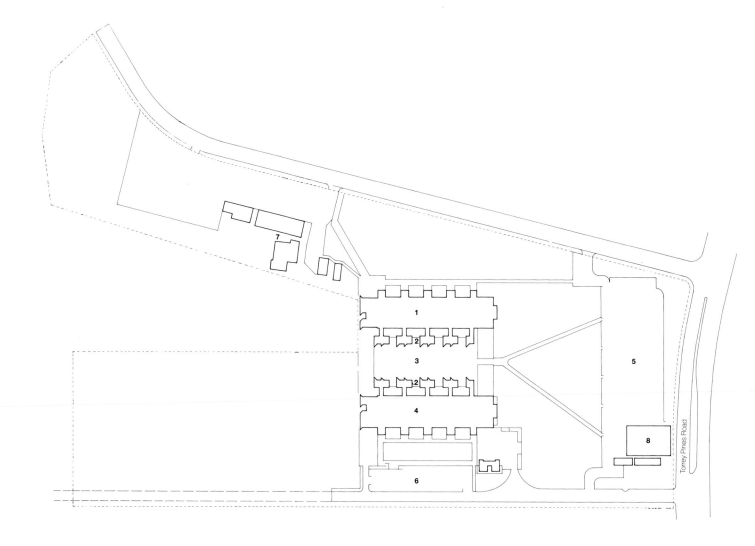

0     100 metres

0     100 yards

**Lower floor plan**
**at laboratory level**

1 laboratory
2 garden
3 office
4 mechanical room
5 incinerator
6 hot and cold
  air supply
7 electrical room

N

0        10 metres
0        30 feet

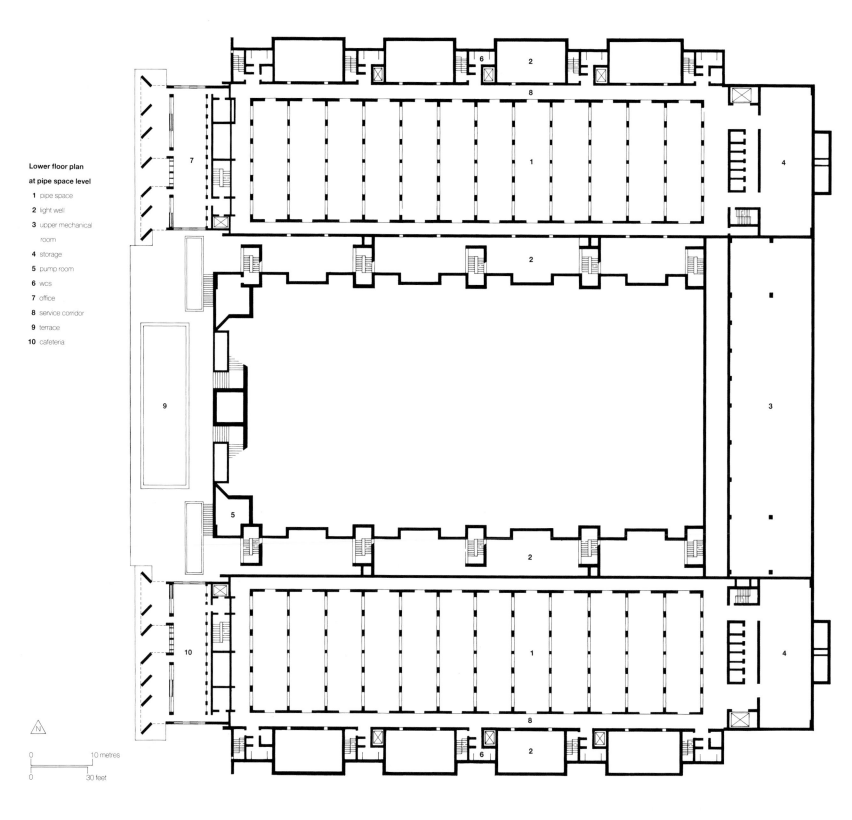

**Lower floor plan
at pipe space level**

**1** pipe space

**2** light well

**3** upper mechanical
room

**4** storage

**5** pump room

**6** wcs

**7** office

**8** service corridor

**9** terrace

**10** cafeteria

N

0 _____ 10 metres

0 _____ 30 feet

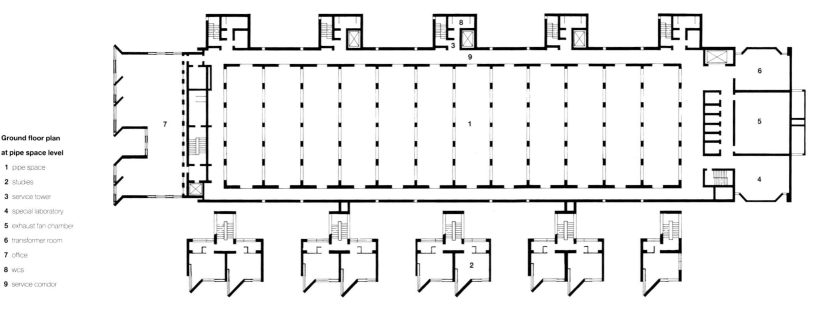

**Ground floor plan
at pipe space level**

1 pipe space
2 studies
3 service tower
4 special laboratory
5 exhaust fan chamber
6 transformer room
7 office
8 wcs
9 service corridor

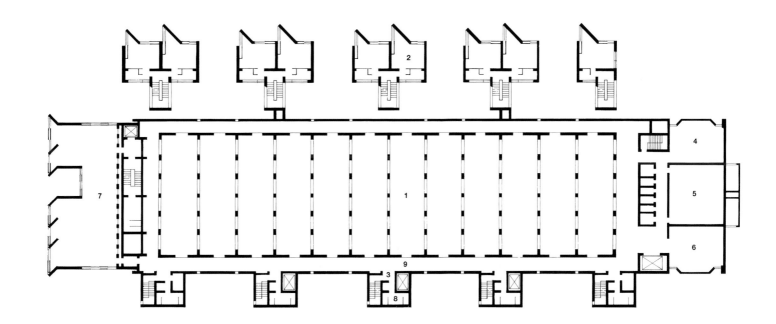

**Ground floor plan**

**at laboratory level**

**1** entry from
  Torrey Pines Road
**2** central court
**3** fountain
**4** portico of studies
**5** light well
**6** laboratory
**7** mechanical
**8** photo lab
**9** library
**10** terrace

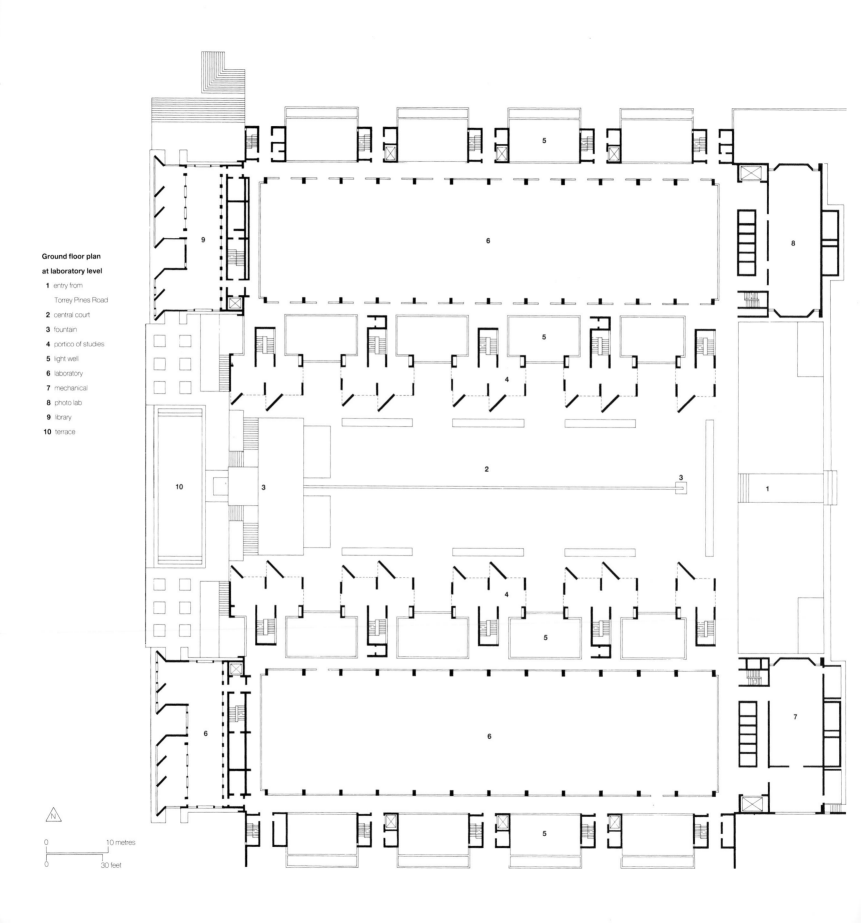

N

0           10 metres

0           30 feet

**Courtyard**

**paving plan**

**1** entry stair from
   Torrey Pines Road

**2** fountain

**3** water line

**4** travertine pavers

**5** portico of studies

**6** light well

**7** stairs to laboratories

**8** terrace overlooking
   the Pacific

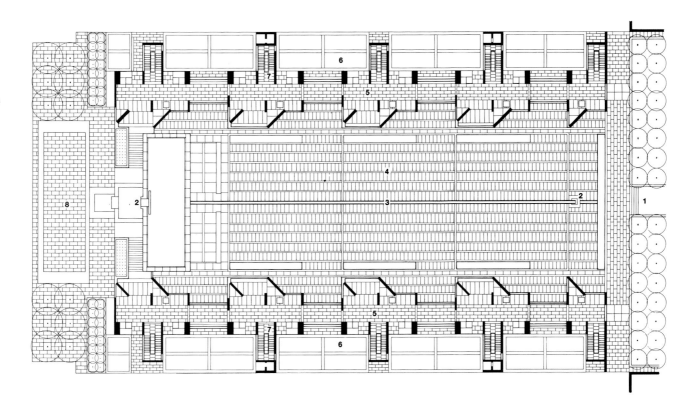

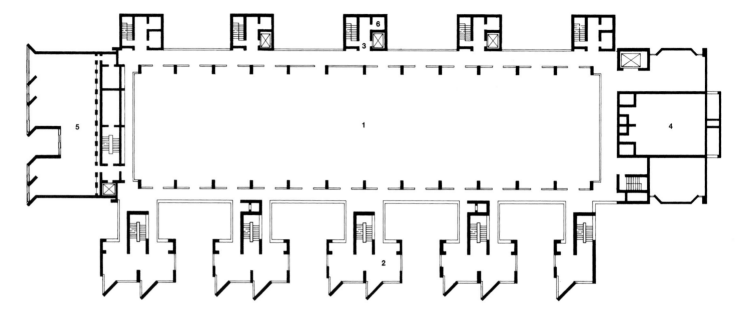

**Upper floor plan
at laboratory level**

**1** laboratory
**2** portico of studies
**3** service tower
**4** mechanical wing
**5** office
**6** wcs

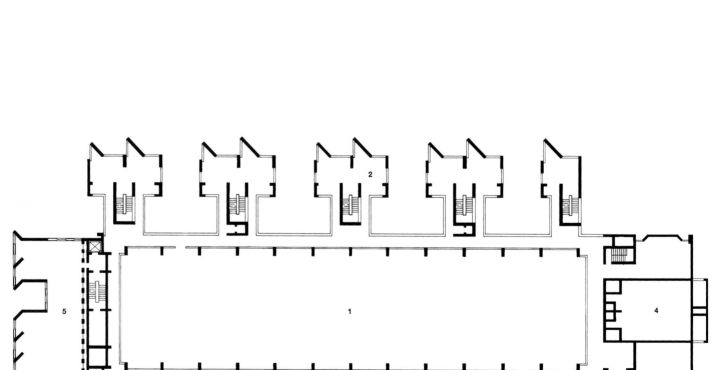

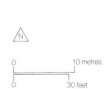

0        10 metres

0        30 feet

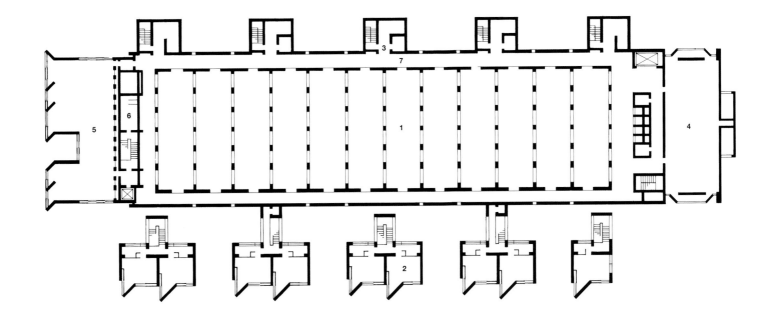

**Upper floor plan**

**at pipe space level**

**1** pipe space

**2** studies

**3** service tower

**4** cooling tower

**5** office

**6** wcs

**7** service corridor

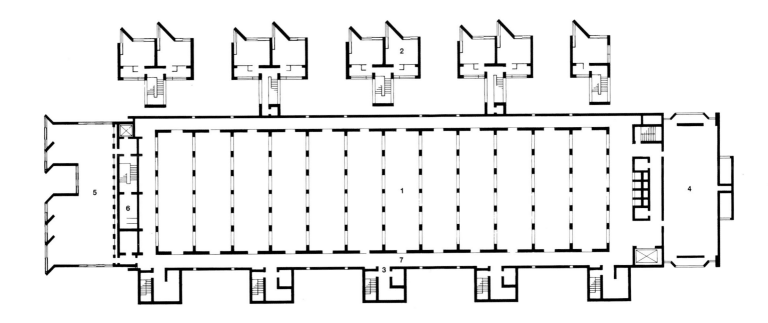

**Section through
laboratories and
central court**

  **1** central court
  **2** portico of studies
  **3** bridge to laboratories
  **4** light well
  **5** laboratory
  **6** interstitial mechanical
      space

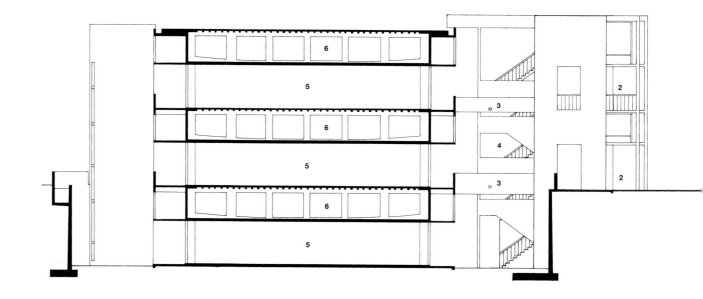

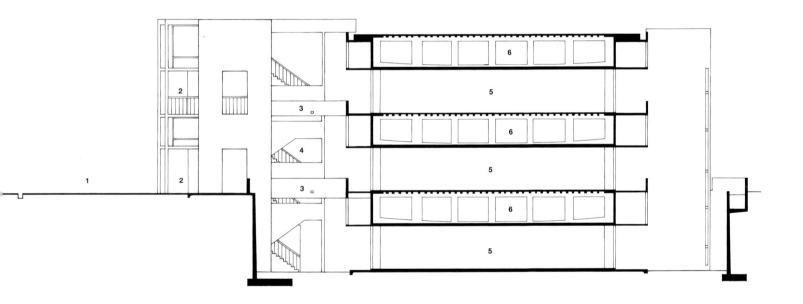

**Section through**

**north office wing**

1 entrance portico

2 office

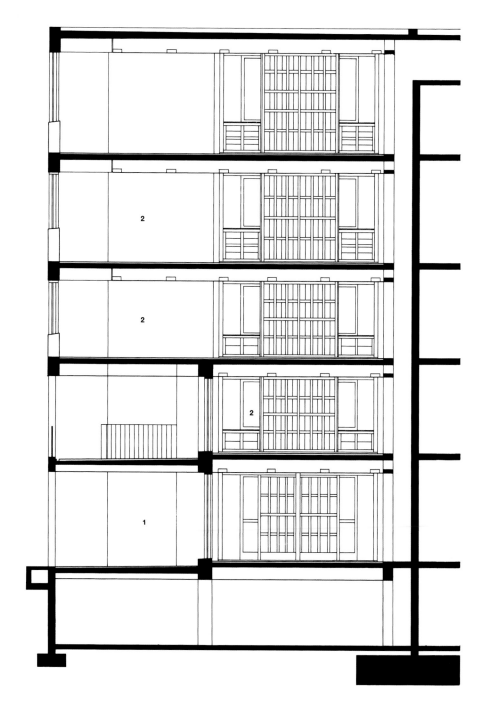

0              3 metres

0              10 feet

Probative detail
section through
sliding teak shutters
in a typical study

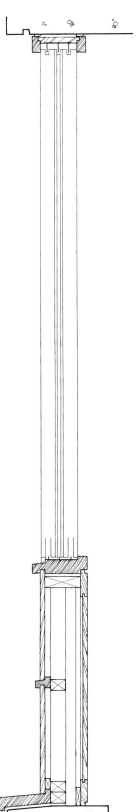

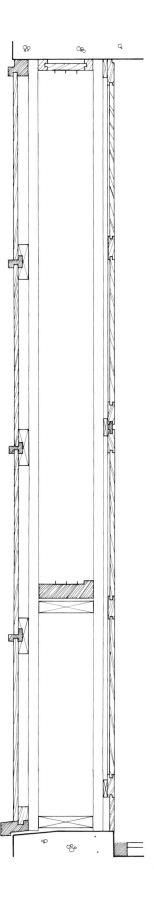

0        200mm

0        6 inches